YOUR PERSONAL CHALLENGE

WITH **DIE-HARD WEALTH** AND

Prosperity

DR. SHARON LEE GRAHAM, D.C.COUN., Th.D.

LET ME CHALLENGE YOU TO CONFRONT ISSUES CONCERNING
WEALTH AND PROSPERITY

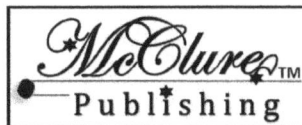

McClure™ Publishing

Tree image by www.123rf.com
Cover Design and Interior Layout by Kathy McClure
McClure Publishing, Inc.
800.659.4908

To order additional copies, please contact
DR. SHARON LEE GRAHAM PRODUCTIONS
http://www.sharonleegraham.com/
and at
www.mcclurepublishing.com

TABLE OF CONTENTS

Page

WILL YOU LET ME CHALLENGE YOU TO FACE YOUR OWN PERSONAL CHALLENGES
WITH DIE-HARD WEALTH AND PROSPERITY?

PURPOSE

The purpose of this workbook is to encourage you to work toward success by providing hands-on instructions and worksheets. This workbook is to be used as a tool to help you work through the process of keeping track of your financial obligations. My desire is to share some information that helped me tremendously, and I believe it will be of value to you.

Another purpose for this workbook is to help you work through issues you might have with the words "wealth" and "prosperity."

In this workbook, I give tips and ideas to stimulate creative juices that will help people face and overcome the challenges that come along with lack and oppression. For anyone who feels it is wrong to be wealthy and prosperous, I ask you to allow me to challenge you to be free from thoughts that being wealthy is not for everyone. Everyone deserves to live a prosperous life.

This workbook is not a get rich quick scheme, neither is it a scam. As a disclaimer, I must tell you that I cannot and I am not guaranteeing that you will become rich. I cannot and I am not guaranteeing that you will become wealthy or prosperous. Your wealth, prosperity and riches depend on what you do with what you have.

INTRODUCTION

This workbook is being composed during the October 1-16, 2013, Government shutdown that affected many, many people financially. I did not participate. I did not change my financial lifestyle. Those who followed my God-given plan did not participate. I caught the vision and then I taught the vision of how to prepare for times of financial turmoil. Individually and collectively you can prepare ahead of the storm. You do not have to wait for federal, state or local entities to come to your rescue. These same entities failed and depended on you for financial help. The financial help given to them came in the form of financial cuts to many of the programs that provided benefits to those in need. Those who were dependent upon the benefits of these programs soon found themselves in a pickle. It pays to have your own.

You will learn how to be accountable for every cent and dollar that comes into your possession. The process involved with learning how to be accountable requires work on your part; this is a necessary and important process. In the end, you will be able to see and appreciate the benefits of this training. You will use the worksheets included in this workbook and enter your own personal data. There are a few supplies needed for this training. You will need a pencil, paper, and calculator (optional), all of your bills, a small pocket size tablet, a will to learn, and the determination to be faithful with completing your assignments in this workbook.

You will become familiar with the principles and tactics I used to launch myself ahead of the game. As you follow the principles contained in this workbook, you will learn what it means to be a good steward and the benefits that come along with good stewardship.

As you practice and apply the principles that I share, become proficient in using them and then teach them to your young people so they can learn accountability early in life; and when they are old, they will not have to depend on you for financial support.

This workbook is not intended to be your average mathematical textbook. This is a one-of-a-kind financial workbook that starts with the basic foundation of honesty and common sense. As a matter of fact, the contents of this workbook will be somewhat different than what you might expect to find in a financial workbook. I am excited to share this information with you.

My desire and prayer for you is that you will know and follow God's plan for your life. His plan is to prosper you in every area of your life.

MY GOAL

My goal for writing this workbook is to see others motivated to reach their goals in the areas of wealth and prosperity. To impart a boost of encouragement, push others forward and cause them to press ahead in the Spirit to the next level where they are supposed to be. I will have reached my goal when I see others become successful as a result of having completed and applied the principles in this workbook.

DEDICATIONS

I am grateful to my family for encouraging me to reach my goal of helping others achieve their desired success in wealth and prosperity.

I would like to thank my granddaughter, Ms. Angelica Graham, for suggesting that I put in writing the things I have taught at the financial seminars. Her desire was that others would have the same opportunity to learn and apply the principles and get the same results as the actual attendees. What a great idea, Angelica. Thank you!

I am grateful for the love and support I received from my daughters, Dr. Yvette Williams and Ms. Mary Graham. These two have great patience; they were my proofreaders. A million thanks to you!

I acknowledge my father, Raymond Boyd, Sr., and my grandmother, Alma Bridgewater, for teaching me the principles I have shared in this workbook. Thank you for the great impartation of wisdom!

I am thankful for the words spoken prophetically over me by my mother, Martha Boyd, when I was very young. I have accomplished, and I am still accomplishing, everything she spoke. I realize God gave her a glimpse of what he had in store for me, and he allowed her to share it with me. Thank you, mom!

GET AN UNDERSTANDING

It is not uncommon for people to have financial challenges. Financial challenges are to be dealt with and deleted. It is vitally important that you understand the meaning of the words I used in the title of this workbook. For example, I used the words "die-hard," "wealth," and "prosperity" for a specific purpose. You can look in the dictionary for the meanings of these words. I am sure you will get the gist of what they mean as you read further into the workbook.

Die-Hard

I used the term "die-hard" because I want the wealth, prosperity and principles that are presented in this workbook to remain a part of your life from this point on. In short, I want your blessings to remain; so, when entities fail, your wealth and prosperity continues.

You deserve the very best of everything on planet earth and you can have it. It is my desire that you have the courage to believe with expectancy and realize that you are in line for the generational blessings

15

that are owed to you. You are important and you deserve the very best. Do you believe that?

You were not created to be beneath; if you believe someone has to be, I have great news for you, you do not have to be the one. You were created to be on top.

<u>Wealth</u>

I used the word "wealth" because wealth plays an important role in the success of our nation and in our personal lives. Some people feel it is a sin to be wealthy. These people have the mighty dollar sign engraved in their mind and have most likely been indoctrinated to believe that they should be poor and that God would be pleased with their poverty. Some people have taken a vow of poverty and believe this pleases God. Maybe their **god** is pleased with their poverty, but the True and Living **God** is not. They think being poor means they are humble, but what it really means is having an unjustifiable lack of understanding concerning the godly principles of obtaining wealth.

It is a blessing to have an abundance of supplies and resources that can be shared or donated to those in need. It is a blessing to have more than enough so you can give to whomever you choose. It would be selfish to only want enough for yourself and your family and not want enough to share. Why struggle and not have enough food, clothing and housing?

16

Why trust in a failing system and beg with your facial expressions? It is not a sin to be wealthy. I have wealth in many areas of my life just as I am prosperous in many areas of my life. For example, I have a wealth of knowledge that causes me to be successful as I conduct business and make wise decisions. It causes me to be safe and avoid danger and enables me to teach others. The desire to obtain a wealth of knowledge is not a sin. List more areas where wealth is not measured by the dollar sign:

1.

2.

3.

4.

5.

Rich

Although the word "rich" is not used in the title of this workbook, it is another word that has been looked upon as a bad word or a word that carries a negative connation by some people; but I am not one of them. I think "rich" is a word fit for kingdom people. What is so bad about being rich? If you think rich only refers to money, you might want to reconsider

17

that the word "rich" refers to more than money, just as wealth means more than money.

Have you ever had a homemade dish that was very flavorful and rich? If you feel being rich is a sin, would you rather have a homemade dish that contains no salt, butter or any other seasonings? Have you heard a lecture that was so informative that you considered it to be rich and powerful? List a few areas in your life where you can exclude money as it pertains to the word "rich" and yet see where you would be better off or more helpful to others if you were rich in that particular area:

1.

2.

3.

4.

5.

Prosperity

The word "prosperity" should be one of our main vocabulary words. When I am assigned a task, I expect to be successful in my accomplishment of that task. I realize that I must start somewhere to begin the task. I must prosper as I go if I intend to successfully complete the task. It is prosperity that causes me to flourish and to be successful.

Learning to maximize your resources, skills, abilities, gifts, talents and callings is vital to your success and wellbeing. Put forth the effort to maximize your full potential in every area of your life. This is called prosperity. Think big. Look for expansion. Expect great. Strive to do your best at whatever you attempt. Expect to feel better tomorrow than you feel today. If you feel better today than you felt yesterday, you are living in prosperity in the area of your health. Your life consists of more than your earthly possessions. Health, happiness, peace, safety, relationships, love and whatever it takes to survive are some of the many important areas of your life where prosperity would make a difference. List other important areas of your life where prosperity would make a big impact:

1.

2.

3.

4.

5.

Having prosperity in those areas mean things are getting better. So, look for the better. When the area of health goes south, life deteriorates and death follows, unless prosperity steps in and healing takes place. When the area of relationships is out of order in your life, bad things follow, unless prosperity intervenes and changes are made.

What about happiness? Happiness is a part of life. Without happiness, life would be sad and some might consider life as being useless. Prosperity is vital to living a successful life. There is nothing bad or immoral about being prosperous and living a life of prosperity.

Beware of people who love pity-parties just to get your sympathy. They hate the word "prosperity." If they prosper, they lose your sympathy and your attention. To prosper means they will have to lift a finger and do something constructive. You might want to consider if these are the people who enhance your prosperity or who pull down the strength of your motivation to prosper. Can you afford to carry even one of them as your bosom buddy?

List areas where you have relinquished control and allowed others to have power over your ability to prosper:

1.

2.

3.

4.

5.

Now that you have listed the areas over which you have relinquished control, give thought to the actions you might take to regain control. Be sensitive and remember the power you gave to others did not happen overnight, be tactful in what you do. When you allow people to have control over your life for so long, they feel at home and comfortable having this kind of control. If they do not have a life of their own, your life becomes their life. Remember, the issue concerns those who have hindered your prosperity. So, list some of the ways you intend to correct these issues and to take back your control so that you can prosper:

1.

2.

3.

4.

5.

PRINCIPLES

The principles that I will share with you are principles I have used for many years and will continue to use. Over the years, I watched my father use some of these principles and I have come to realize that they have become a vital part of my life.

The basic foundation for all of the principles that my father taught me was built upon learning to take responsibility, being accountable, and being honest. I learned the importance of keeping record of my bills, such as due dates and dates my bills are paid.

As you read, you will see many principles I have learned to live by. I believe you will be helped by them if you implement them in your life.

I DO NOT FOOLISHLY SPEND EVERY PENNY I EARN

Walking around with all of your money in your possession is not wise. Doing this makes it easy to nickel and dime every penny away before you realize what you have done. Now you have no money left, your bills are due, you have no clue as to where your money went, and you are left unable to give an account of your spending. What would you do? Would you beg or borrow to meet your financial obligations? You could have put money aside to pay your bills. If you and an acquaintance have the same amount of money and equal bill obligations, would you approach that person and ask for money? If that person refused to give you money, would you be angry? I have seen people become angry over such nonsense. How can someone become angry over what does not belong to them? Easy, I guess. This type of event should never occur, but it does.

Budgeting is very important. Later, you will give an account of every penny you spend, down to the cup of coffee you buy. If you follow the assignments given in this workbook, you will become a better steward and manager of your finances. Teach your young people to manage their money and to recognize the importance of keeping track of how much comes in, how much goes out, and how much is saved. Remember, this is not a get-rich-quick scheme. It takes time to build. Keep building.

I DO NOT BORROW

My grandmother taught me not to borrow. She said if you borrow an iron from someone and you break it, you will have to spend money to replace it and you still don't have an iron. She said it is better to buy your own iron. When she told me that, I do not think I was old enough to use an iron, but as you can tell, what she said stayed with me. When teaching your young people to be independent, and they appear to disregard your

24

instructions, be patient; sooner or later, they will remember what you taught them.

Borrowing should not become a generational addiction. If your children observe your continued habit of borrowing, they will do the same. If you constantly borrow and fail to pay back, they will do the same. If they see you being immoral, you are their example and your example is teaching them to do the same. Would you expect them to do differently?

I DO KEEP MY WORD

When any type of purchase is made on credit, you are liable for payment. This would include the purchase of a house, car, clothes, utilities or any other purchase you can think of. You are held accountable for payment when you rent an apartment, vehicle, furniture or any other rentable item. You are liable when you give your word, make a pledge or sign a contract. Do you keep your word? If you do not, how do you expect prosperity to come your way? Prosperity might come your way and pass you by because of your lack of honesty and integrity.

I DO PAY MY DEBTS

How can you buy a pair of shoes but cannot pay your rent or cannot pay the person you borrowed from? Where is your conscience? I know this statement might seem to be a little harsh, but it's the harsh facts that bring us to the reality of how important it is to be disciplined in financial matters. Remember, the basic foundation for all of the principles that were taught to me by my father was built upon learning to take responsibility, being accountable, and being honest. This workbook will show you how to put these principles into action. Another harsh fact that must be addressed is when you continue to borrow and never pay back, that is wicked. The Good Book said it!

I AM ACCOUNTABLE

If for any reason you are unable to pay your debt on time, do you run away or pretend it does not exist? Be accountable. Face your debtor, in person or over the phone, and give an explanation. As you carefully budget, follow the worksheets in this workbook, and faithfully use your pocket size tablet, you should be able to avoid overspending. You want to get to the point of being able to save for emergencies, entertainment and other things on your bucket list. To get to this point, you will need to discipline yourself concerning your spending habits. You will need to track your spending in order to recognize any wasteful spending. To be successful, you will have to do some work. I did it and so can you.

I AM HONEST AND FAITHFUL

Try taking inventory of how you operate in business and in everyday dealings with others. Honesty and faithfulness are major players on your team. Let them help you win the battle against poverty and lack. Let them usher wealth and riches to your door.

I DO HAVE A WEALTHY MINDSET

Wealthy people view wealth differently than those who are not. Wealthy people manage what they have. I have found that people who live in lack have more than they realize. The majority of the time they do not keep track of what comes in or what goes out, which means they fail to manage what they have. The seriousness of not being a good manager of your own finances causes lack. Remember, whatever you fail to manage will most likely fall through the cracks unnoticed until an emergency arises. Let's not allow this to happen to us.

I DO NOT COSIGN

Have you ever had someone constantly in your face cheesing until you loan them money or cosign for them? Then, after they get the money or you cosign, they act as though you are an alien, they do not know you and they try to avoid you. What happened to the cheesing and that all-in-your-face stuff? I do not cosign. I learned that from The Good Book. Borrowing, loaning and cosigning has ended many friendships and it is not a good practice. If you cosign for someone, you are tagged with liabilities. If you cosigned for them to buy a house or a boat and they do not pay for it, do you want that house or that boat? Were you prepared to make that purchase? If they fail to pay, it is now your responsibility. Does that make you happy?

I DO GIVE THE TITHE (10%) AND I FILE MY INCOME TAX RETURN

God is to be number one in all things. Seek God, his kingdom and his righteousness first, and then the wealth and prosperity you desire will follow. We render to Caesar the things that are Caesar's. Why not render to God the things that are God's? God will not withhold any good thing from those who love him. Do not cheat God by keeping his tithes (10%). If you are struggling, is it because you are paying the price of withholding that portion that belongs to God? Do not cheat Uncle Sam by avoiding your taxes; there will be a price to pay to the Internal Revenue Service. Are you cheating Uncle Sam? I learned these principles from The Good Book, too. I am sure you know by now, The Good Book is the Best Book…. The Bible!

List other principles that would be beneficial to building wealth and prosperity:

1.

2.

3.

4.

5.

THE WEALTH CULTURE

I must say, taking on the task of changing a culture is a difficult one, especially when the culture you are trying to change is one of negativity and poverty, and that has been etched in stone and followed religiously throughout the years. Some people are comfortable with a familiar culture regardless of the negative impact, and will refuse to leave it behind for a better way of life. People tend to fear the new because they are accustomed to a certain way of living. As comfortable as it may feel living in the realm of an old culture, I believe trying an unfamiliar, new culture that brings a better way of life will prove to be worth any discomfort experienced during the process of change. The culture that changes the lives of people from poverty and lack to a culture of wealth and prosperity is a positive and beneficial culture.

You can be delivered from the culture of poverty. One way to be delivered is to transform your mind from the poverty mentality to a culture of freedom from begging and borrowing.

There is a false implication that has been passed along that tends to steer generation after generation into the way of believing it is wrong to be wealthy when in fact people in general do not understand what it really

29

means to be wealthy. The word wealthy is not a cuss word. I would say it is a blessed word if you use it right.

I would like to say a few things to those who feel it is not God's will for them to be wealthy and ask a few questions in hope of introducing new thoughts in the process of their thinking. If you are employed, evidently your employer is wealthy or rich enough to employ you. How would you like for them to go broke so that you are without employment? The consequences of this are far reaching. You could possibly end up in the unemployment line; at the public aid office applying for a link card and section eight housing; or in line at a charity seeking shelter, groceries and clothing. We might even see you standing at the exit of an expressway selling peanuts or washing car windshields as people try to avoid you. Do not get me wrong, I give credit to those who sell peanuts, fruits and other items along the sides of the expressways, if they have the required license to do so. At least they are trying to make a living; I am not putting them down for that. Better yet, you might say you would never do any of those things, and that you would never be a street peddler and that might be true. But, would you beg and borrow from friends and family or depend on others and feel they are obligated to take care of you just because they have what you need? If so, you might as well stand on the street and hold up your sign asking for money if you are going to beg and depend on others instead of trying to get a job and work for your living. Do you think being poor and living a life of poverty is okay? People will eventually avoid you and find being around you pulls them down. Do you realize what a burden this might cause for others? Your culture has much to do with your success or the lack thereof. Is it time for a culture change?

THE WEALTH CULTURE REQUIRES A NEW WAY OF THINKING

You can choose to change your culture by changing your way of thinking. You can change your way of thinking by seeking and receiving an education that pulls your level of thinking to a higher realm and by making the necessary environmental changes. If your desire is to improve, you might need to connect with someone who can help you make the improvements you desire. If you have the desire for change, and if you make a step in that direction, things will start to happen for you.

DO NOT ACCEPT GUILT

Do not fall into the guilt trap if you are happy and you have plenty. Where does this guilt come from? Who have you been listening to? Who have you been watching and who have you been hanging around? If the company you keep encourages you to be poor, are they poor? Are they satisfied with their level of wealth and prosperity or the lack thereof? Take a good observation. Sometimes a change of environment is required.

31

Are you living from paycheck to paycheck? If you are, do you feel this is the way you have to live, and are you okay with living this way? If you are not okay with living from paycheck to paycheck, may I encourage you to start a budget?

I believe having more than enough is the way to go, but how about you? If you desire to reach the level of having more than enough of everything, how do you get to that level?

GETTING OFF THE SYSTEM

For those who have had to receive assistance from local, state or federal agencies but were able to get off the system and are no longer receiving their assistance, I am sure it took a change of mind and way of thinking to make the transition to freedom. You can do whatever you set your mind to. Your mind is powerful, use it!

Here is an in-your-face revelation:

1. Young person on the system – dropped out of school – no job
2. Same young person – now has children – no spouse
3. Same young person – age 45 – now has grandchildren
4. Same young person – now old – sitting at home depending on the system, children, grandchildren and others.
5. Same young person – never attempted to get an education or get a job.
6. Same young person – was poor – now old – still poor.

If you are poor and on the system and take no action to better yourself, to get off of it while you are young, you will be stuck on the system and remain poor in your old age. Get up, get busy, and use your mind while you still have an opportunity. Seek to surround yourself with others who have a proven track record of accomplishing something valuable in life. Check with your local community college for adult continuing education or other community agencies that will introduce you to the proper resources to help you with job training and placement opportunities.

List some ways that will help you prosper now and even more so in your later years:

1.

2.

3.

4.

5.

6.

BEING COVERED

DO YOU HAVE THE NECESSARY INSURANCE COVERAGES?

<u>LIFE INSURANCE</u>

There are various types of life insurances. Do you know which insurances you need? What about the person who does not believe they need life insurance and feel they have the right to rely on someone else to bury them and bear the burden of the expense? What about the person who refuses to pay premiums for life insurance because they will not get the money after they die and they do not want to leave any money for someone else to enjoy? What is your take on this, or are you the person who does not believe you need life insurance?

List reasons why insurance is important:

1.

2.

35

3.

4.

5.

List reasons why insurance is not necessary:

1.

2.

3.

If you have a spouse or children, what happens financially if there are no insurance policies when needed? Are you thinking that someone else will use their hard earned cash to pay for your burial and the burial of your family? Maybe you should have a meeting of the minds to find out who will take care of your expenses, if you do not intend to purchase insurance to cover your responsibilities. Insurances are not free. They require premiums that must be paid on time. If you refuse to pay the premiums to have the insurance you need, why would you feel others are obligated to pay their own insurance premiums and then pay for your burial expenses? If you cannot afford insurance at this time, do not be discouraged. The purpose of this workbook is to help you budget so you can get the coverage you need. (Some life insurance policies depreciate when you reach a certain age. Do you have enough money set aside to cover your burial expenses?)

MEDICAL INSURANCE

Health insurance, dental and vision insurance are important and are usually offered upon employment. If you or your dependents are sick and in need of medical treatment and you have no coverage, who do you think should pay the medical bills if you are unable to do so? Will the medical institution turn your bills over to a collections attorney? If you are unable to get coverage because you cannot afford it, keep reading and purpose in your heart that you will budget and practice principles that will help you manage your finances so you can reach the point of fitting medical coverage into your budget. Remember, nothing is free and changes might occur when political parties change.

Eventually, you might want to check into long-term care insurance. Do not forget Medicare insurance when you reach the eligible age.

RENTERS AND HOMEOWNERS INSURANCE

If you are buying property, the seller or mortgage company wants their money if something happens to the property and will require that you purchase insurance to protect their interest. If the property is damaged or destroyed, you must have it repaired or replaced. Insurance is necessary and comes in handy. You are responsible for the payment of the property even if you are sick. There is coverage that pays the mortgage if you are sick and unable to work. For those who are renting, you need insurance to cover your own personal property. You cannot depend on the landlord.

CAR INSURANCE

Do you drive or allow your children or others to drive without insurance coverage? What happens if there is an accident? When vehicular damage, property damage, bodily harm, or death occurs as a result of your uninsured vehicle being involved in an accident, who pays when law suits are filed against you? All states require drivers to have some type of automobile insurance. Some car dealerships will not allow you to drive off of the lot without proof of coverage after purchasing a new vehicle. Follow the principles of being accountable and responsible. Budgeting will help you reach the point of including the coverage you need. It might take a while, just stick with it.

Make your own list of insurances not mentioned above:

1. _____

2. _____

3. _____

4. _____

5. _____

NOTE: I do not sell, work for or represent any insurance company, nor am I a spokesperson for any insurance company.

DO YOU HAVE A RETIREMENT PLAN?

Retirement time comes around faster than you realize. Here are a few questions to think about concerning retirement. Does your employer offer a retirement plan? Are you putting extra money into the plan? Do you have a retirement plan outside of your place of employment? It is not a bad idea to start your young people a retirement plan as soon as possible; they are never too young! You can retire and live comfortably if you plan.

DID YOU KNOW SOCIAL SECURITY IS A SUPPLEMENT TO YOUR RETIREMENT PLAN?

People have said they are going to retire and get their social security in belief that the amount they expect to receive will be sufficient to live on for the balance of their days. Upon further conversation, I find out they have no retirement plan. Be advised, social security is not a retirement plan, it is a supplement to your retirement plan.

DO YOU HAVE SAVINGS/CHECKING/ETC.?

If you are on the system, you are not allowed to stay on the system if your savings or checking accounts exceed a certain amount. What about CDs, money market accounts, savings bonds, annuities, IRAs, Christmas club accounts, and other types of savings? You cannot freely have as much money as you want in all of these if you are on the system. Supposedly, you are on the system because you cannot afford these savings. Being on the system is being in bondage. You will not be able to accumulate these savings as long as you are in bondage. You need to be able to save and manage your money if you intend to tap into the die-hard wealth and prosperity I am talking about in this workbook. When job or educational opportunities knock, seize the opportunity.

DO YOU HAVE A WILL/TRUST/POWER OF ATTORNEY, ETC.?

Some people feel they have nothing of value and that it would be useless to have a will, trust or powers of attorney. I have found a lot of people have more than they realize. If you are unable to write checks to pay your bills, to speak for yourself, or to tell the doctors your desires, who will be able to do those things for you if you have not designated anyone to have the powers of attorney? It might be a good idea to talk with a legal professional before making the decision to pass on such important business matters.

ARE YOUR IMPORTANT PAPERS IN ORDER AND ACCESSIBLE?

Have you ever searched for important papers, you began to sweat and you still cannot remember where you placed them? You might consider setting up a file and organizing it so you can quickly access the papers you need in times of emergency or other business situations. Just think of the panic others would face if they had to search for your important papers if you were unavailable or unable to tell them exactly where to locate them. Have a plan in place and notify those who have a need to know.

List some important documents that you might need to have handy:

1.

2.

3.

4.

<u>DO YOU HAVE AN EMERGENCY FUND?</u>

When emergencies knock at your door, do you have money set aside to get you through the emergency, or do you go from person to person in an effort to collect the funds you need? People are not to be used as your emergency fund. Do not be surprised when people tend to avoid you because you appear to be needy all of the time. Think of the times you spent money for non-essential items. Think about the shoes you bought, even though you had a dozen pairs you had never worn. Think of the unnecessary spending you do on a continuous basis. Think about changing your habit of unnecessary spending and start placing that money in an emergency fund account. Think of how great you might feel when you are financially stable and no longer begging and borrowing. Later in the workbook, in the "EXAMPLES" chapter, we will discuss "CARRYOVER." Stay tuned.

FROM POVERTY TO WEALTH

I am sure most wealthy people have great stories to tell about their wealth and success. The greatest stories are probably the ones that concern the history of how they became wealthy and successful, of their lean days and the struggles they had to overcome. They would probably tell about the sacrifices they made to get to where they are today. Some would say they became wealthy because of an inheritance or because they were the beneficiary of an insurance policy; nevertheless, each has a story.

If you had the opportunity to ask questions of wealthy people, what would you ask? Let us venture out and ask questions and find answers.

QUESTION: How does it feel to be wealthy?

ANSWER: This person said being wealthy made them feel great; but the feeling of having enough material goods to share with others was even greater and that having enough love, peace, joy and happiness to share mean more than riches, silver or gold. They acknowledged that all of these things, material riches and emotional riches, are needed to make up wealth and riches; without them, people are broke. They also said you can have all of the money, material goods, wealth, friends, family, and anything else in the world, but if you do not have your health and happiness you are broke. This person acknowledged they are blessed to have good health, happiness and wealth and it is all because they put God first in everything they do.

QUESTION: Were you always wealthy?

ANSWER: One person said they always had a rich mindset and a wealth mentality. This mindset was the result of their home training. Although they had lean days at home, the mindset of wealth and riches was the normal way of thinking in their house. They were taught to never beg or borrow. This was a rule that became law in their household. They did not have the money or the material goods at the time they were growing up, but they always felt rich. They always felt they could have whatever they wanted and that nothing could stop them from achieving a set goal. They said wealth does not refer to money and material goods only. They viewed having riches and wealth as a normal way of life. They had a rich mindset and a wealth mentality first and it finally manifested to where it became tangible for them to see and to touch; in other words, they believed it, they thought it, and then they received it.

QUESTION: How did you become wealthy?

ANSWER: One young person received an inheritance of property and money from their grandparents and their parents helped them manage

44

the inheritance. Since this person was young at the time of the inheritance, they believe they would have spent foolishly and would have lost the property if proper guidance had not been given by their parents.

Financial training and oversight is very important. If you have finances and property and you do not know how to manage them, it is highly advised that you consult a professional for assistance. It would also be a good idea for you to get some financial training so you can understand how your business is being handled. It is less costly to hire a professional to help you manage your inheritance than it is to lose it.

Another person said they were not born into a wealthy family. They worked hard to get what they have and they learned to manage their earnings and to sacrifice some of the things they wanted for pleasure. It was not easy for them to watch others splurge on pleasurable goods and living the fast life. Although the fast life was tempting, this person did not take that route, but saved for the future. Resisting the urge to splurge paid off. The one who splurged was the one who needed the cash later, but there was none.

There must be balance. When you work hard, you need to enjoy the fruit of the labor of your hands without wasteful spending. The sacrifices that were made paid off when hard times came. It was like saving for a rainy day. The person who works hard, saves and learns how to manage their money is the person who will be prepared for rainy days. The person who gives freely and knows how to say "no" when necessary has wisdom and the power to prosper.

QUESTION: What can I do to become wealthy?

ANSWER: That is an excellent question. Dr. Graham has created a workbook that gives principles and examples of how to start from scratch and move into a place of wealth. This workbook is hands-on with your bills and shows you how to manage your finances. This workbook is a good tool to use when teaching your children to manage their finances. Remember, it is not always the amount of money you have, it is all about how you handle it. This workbook is most unusual because it challenges you concerning your own personal finances, not the finances of someone else. Do you want to be successful with your money? How diligent are you willing to work toward making the change that is necessary for your financial success? Dr. Graham has taught numerous four-month, hands-on seminars concerning finances and has placed that information in a workbook. The title of the financial workbook is, "DIE-HARD WEALTH AND PROSPERITY." It is your personal challenge workbook, and it will be on the best sellers list real soon!

After the interviews, I have concluded that it is a wonderful thing to be wealthy. A lot of people desire to be wealthy. If you are one of them, I have a few questions to ask you. Along with the desire to be rich and wealthy, are you willing to walk in the shoes of a wealthy person? Are you aware of the times they have to turn off their communications or leave their residence in order to have rest from beggars and people they have not heard from in decades? Are you ready to have people you barely know asking of you just because? Are you aware of the danger of the "I have arrived" attitude if you are wealthy? Did you know you can lose your wealth if you don't stay on top of things or if you become lazy? Did you know wealthy people do not get their wealth and sit down, but continue to be involved in the areas that concern their wealth? Are you willing to do what it takes, or at least what they did to get to where they are? Are you willing to make sacrifices and to resist the temptations of buying everything you think you want just because you have the money? In order to have some money, do you realize you cannot spend all you have and not go broke? Are you willing to deal honestly in business and follow godly principles? Are you willing to have a heart after God, to love people and to share? Are you willing to help those in need by giving them a fishing pole, some bate and teaching them how to fish? Finally, are you willing to use the word "NO" when necessary?

P.S. One last thought-provoking question for you: Will you accept the challenge to change where change is needed?

I realize the questions I pose seem to be on the negative side, but there are two sides of the coin and I want to show both sides. Wisdom, knowledge and understanding are necessary keys for the wealthy. Believe me, the grace and wisdom of God are necessary if you are answering "YES" to the above questions. Some people cannot handle the wealth; some cannot handle the stress and pressures that come along with the wealth. I would rather be wealthy any day. I will repeat it over and over, "I WOULD RATHER BE WEALTHY ANY DAY!" God has wealth written on me and in me and He helps me handle it all; let Him do the same for you. It is the Father's pleasure to give us the kingdom and I receive the kingdom and everything in it!

I pray that you receive the wisdom of God to be a good manager over the finances He has for you, and that you will never have to beg, borrow, steal nor suffer lack. I pray that God will grant you continued health, safety and peace!

Sincerely,

DR SLG

SUPPLIES NEEDED

Paper

Pencil

Calculator

All Bills & Financial Obligations

Pay Stubs & a list of all Income

A small pocket size tablet

INSTRUCTIONS AND WORKSHEETS

<u>INSTRUCTIONS</u>

The top right portion of your worksheet is to be dated and used for listing all income, child support, spousal support and any other form of scheduled income, and to add the carryover total from the previous month, and to subtract tithes (10%).

Carryover is the amount of money left over after all financial obligations have been taken care of. Do not be discouraged if your carryover is showing a minus. As you become more disciplined in managing your finances, the minus will eventually change to a plus.

After you have completed the above instructions, you will have a total. The total is the amount of money you have to work with.

51

WORKSHEET

DATE:_____

(Full-Time Job Income) $_____

(Part-Time Job) $_____

(Other Income) $_____

(Subtotal) $_____

(Subtract Tithes-10%) $_____

(Subtotal) $_____

(Add last month's Carryover) $_____

(TOTAL) $_____

This sheet is an example of what the top right portion of your worksheet should look like. You might need to adjust the amount of lines to fit your specific need.

INSTRUCTIONS

Now that you have completed the top right portion of your worksheet, you will begin using the remainder of your worksheet to list your financial obligations. You will start this list using the left side of your worksheet.

As you sort through your financial obligations, which we will now call bills, be sure to take into consideration the number of pay days or the number of times you receive your income each month. If you get paid once a month and your additional income is received around the same time, you will need one worksheet. If you get paid twice a month or your additional income is received a few weeks later, you will need two worksheets, etc. You will be able to determine the number of sheets required as you go along.

List your bills according to their due dates. Pay those that are due now first. In this same section, list estimated amounts for groceries, personal necessities, emergencies, and other expenses you might incur.

54

When you estimate your grocery bill or any other bill, be sure to enter the date you expect to go shopping and the actual amount spent as paid.

Look at your list of bills and determine which bills you want to pay at this time and deduct that amount from the total shown in the top right corner of the worksheet.

If you are not paying all of your bills at this time, write in the amounts and due dates for the bills you will pay later. Place an "X" next to the bills that are paid.

The money you have left over, after deducting total bills paid from the total at the top right portion of the page, is to be written at the bottom right side of your worksheet (the amount might be a minus, but that will change). This money becomes your carryover and will be added to the carryover section at the top right portion of your next worksheet.

While trying to become financially stable, I found it helpful just paying only the bills that were due and placing the extra money in my carryover. By placing the extra money in my carryover, my totals grew each month and it felt like I was getting a raise each time I completed my worksheet. The students who followed my plan began to accumulate so much extra; they began to draw from the carryover to open savings accounts and investments, as well as pay off some of those nagging debts. The carryover can eventually be used to obtain those things you thought you could never afford. Do you remember earlier in the workbook I mentioned retirement funds outside of work, extra insurances and other items that seemed out of reach? The carryover will help you reach those things. The carryover helped me reach many, many extras. I paid only the bills that were due. (I am not speaking concerning credit card payments and other bills that charge interest. If you are able to do so, you might want to pay extra on those because of the interest factor.)

WORKSHEET

(List bills – amount due – date due – amount paid – date paid)

	Amount Due	_Date Due_	_Amount Paid_	_Date Paid_
Rent/Mortgage	$		$	
Renter's/Homeowner's Insurance	$		$	
Electric	$		$	
Gas	$		$	
Car Payment	$		$	
Auto Insurance	$		$	
Credit Card	$		$	
Groceries (estimated)	$		$	
Transportation (estimated)	$		$	
Necessities (estimated)	$		$	
Beauty or barbershop (estimated)	$		$	
Entertainment (estimated)	$		$	
Items from Pocket Size Tablet	$		$	

TOTAL ABOVE: $_____   TOTAL BILLS PAID: $_____   CARRYOVER: $_____

This sheet is an example of what the center portion of your worksheet should look like. Adjust the amount of items and name them to fit your specific need. You will use one worksheet per payday. The "CARRYOVER" is the last entry on the worksheet and is located on the bottom right side.

INSTRUCTIONS FOR YOUR POCKET SIZE TABLET

Your pocket size tablet will prove to be a necessary tool in the budgeting process. You will use it to keep track of your daily spending. The success of your budget will be based on how faithfully you enter each purchase you make. This part of the process takes discipline. You can do it. You will be glad you took the challenge in the long run.

We tend to spend loose change and give little thought as to how much we actually spend each day. Sometimes we spend money and cannot give an account as to what we bought. Did we really need what we bought? The answer to that question will be found in the pocket size tablet.

Begin to list every transaction that requires you to spend money, whether cash, credit or debit card. For example:

1 cup coffee - $2.00	2 donuts - $.90	1 newspaper - $1.25	car/gas - $33.00
1 bag potato chips - $1.25	1 roll toilet paper - $1.25	1 book - $17.00	1 dinner - $35.00
1 birthday card - $5.99	1 movie rental - $5.00	bus/train fare - $5.00	2 CDs - $34.00

Choose a date to start tracking your spending. The date you choose should coincide with your worksheet so that you will be able to add your week or two weeks of spending, from your pocket size tablet, to your worksheet. The pages in your pocket size tablet should be dated. If possible, list your spending for the day on one page so you can see how much you spend per day. (Remember, you will use one worksheet per payday.) After you have totaled the week or two weeks of spending in your pocket size tablet, you are now ready to enter the dollar amount and the date. The first dollar amount is your estimation of how much you anticipate spending. Your estimation should be entered before you start spending and before entries are made in your pocket size tablet. The due date is the date you begin tracking your spending in the pocket size tablet. The amount paid is the actual amount you spent for the week or two weeks. The date paid is the last day you tracked your spending in the pocket size tablet.

After a review of your spending, you should be able to see where your money has gone and possibly come up with ways to adjust your spending, such as buying certain items in bulk instead of making a single purchase. Buying items such as tissue, soap and potato chips in bulk is much cheaper than buying them one at a time. You can make a comparison by recording and adding the amount you paid for single purchases and then buy bulk and record that amount, compare and see the savings. What will you do with the amount you saved by buying bulk? You will place it in your carryover. Do not get too out of control with your spending just because you have cut a few corners. The extra money you have left over goes into your carryover.

SAMPLE WORKSHEET   DATE: _____

(Full-Time Job Income) $_____

(Part-Time Job) $_____

(Other Income) $_____

(Subtotal) $_____

(Subtract Tithes-10%) $_____

(Subtotal) $_____

(Add last month's Carryover) $_____

(TOTAL) $_____

	Amount Due	Date Due	Amount Paid	Date Paid
Rent/Mortgage	$_____	_____	$_____	_____
Renter's/Homeowner's Insurance	$_____	_____	$_____	_____
Electric	$_____	_____	$_____	_____
Gas	$_____	_____	$_____	_____
Car Payment	$_____	_____	$_____	_____
Auto Insurance	$_____	_____	$_____	_____
Credit Card	$_____	_____	$_____	_____
Groceries (estimated)	$_____	_____	$_____	_____
Transportation (estimated)	$_____	_____	$_____	_____
Necessities (estimated)	$_____	_____	$_____	_____
Beauty or barbershop (estimated)	$_____	_____	$_____	_____
Entertainment (estimated)	$_____	_____	$_____	_____
Items from Pocket Size Tablet	$_____	_____	$_____	_____

TOTAL ABOVE: $_____   TOTAL BILLS PAID: $_____   CARRYOVER: $_____

(A sample of what your worksheet should look like)

60

Again, you should have a worksheet for each payday. Once you get the gist of budgeting, you can adjust your worksheet to include only the bills you want to pay out of the first check of the month, then use the next worksheet to list the bills you want to pay out of the next paycheck; however, the outlined setup for the upper right hand portion and the last line of the worksheet remains the same for each worksheet.

Be faithful to your budget. Be sure to enter every purchase in your pocket size tablet. The name of the game is to see how much money you can add to your carryover after your financial obligations have been met. Remember, once your carryover is overflowing richly, take some of it to start your emergency fund if you do not have one, or to purchase needed insurances or retirement funds. You should be able to make the determination as to where your carryover is most needed and would be most beneficial.

Teach your young people how to budget and how to be prosperous. This workbook is a great tool to get them started.

PRACTICE WORKSHEET

DATE:_____

INCOME (_____) $_____

INCOME (_____) $_____

INCOME (_____) $_____

(Subtotal) $_____

(Subtract Tithes-10%) $_____

(Subtotal) $_____

(Add last month's Carryover) $_____

(TOTAL) $_____

	Amount Due	*Date Due*	*Amount Paid*	*Date Paid*
_____	$_____	_____	$_____	_____
_____	$_____	_____	$_____	_____
_____	$_____	_____	$_____	_____
_____	$_____	_____	$_____	_____
_____	$_____	_____	$_____	_____
_____	$_____	_____	$_____	_____
_____	$_____	_____	$_____	_____
Groceries (estimated)	$_____	_____	$_____	_____
Transportation (estimated)	$_____	_____	$_____	_____
Necessities (estimated)	$_____	_____	$_____	_____
Beauty or barbershop (estimated)	$_____	_____	$_____	_____
Entertainment (estimated)	$_____	_____	$_____	_____
Items from Pocket Size Tablet	$_____	_____	$_____	_____

TOTAL ABOVE: $_____   TOTAL BILLS PAID: $_____   CARRYOVER: $_____

PRACTICE WORKSHEET

DATE:_____

INCOME (_____) $_____

INCOME (_____) $_____

INCOME (_____) $_____

(Subtotal) $_____

(Subtract Tithes-10%) $_____

(Subtotal) $_____

(Add last month's Carryover) $_____

(TOTAL) $_____

	Amount Due	_Date Due_	_Amount Paid_	_Date Paid_
_____	$_____	_____	$_____	_____
_____	$_____	_____	$_____	_____
_____	$_____	_____	$_____	_____
_____	$_____	_____	$_____	_____
_____	$_____	_____	$_____	_____
_____	$_____	_____	$_____	_____
_____	$_____	_____	$_____	_____
_____	$_____	_____	$_____	_____
_____	$_____	_____	$_____	_____
Necessities (estimated)	$_____	_____	$_____	_____
Beauty or barbershop (estimated)	$_____	_____	$_____	_____
Entertainment (estimated)	$_____	_____	$_____	_____
Items from Pocket Size Tablet	$_____	_____	$_____	_____

TOTAL ABOVE: $_____   TOTAL BILLS PAID: $_____   CARRYOVER: $_____

PRACTICE WORKSHEET

DATE:_____

INCOME (_____) $_____

INCOME (_____) $_____

INCOME (_____) $_____

(Subtotal) $_____

(Subtract Tithes-10%) $_____

(Subtotal) $_____

(Add last month's Carryover) $_____

(TOTAL) $_____

	Amount Due	_Date Due_	_Amount Paid_	_Date Paid_
_____	$_____	_____	$_____	_____
_____	$_____	_____	$_____	_____
_____	$_____	_____	$_____	_____
_____	$_____	_____	$_____	_____
_____	$_____	_____	$_____	_____
_____	$_____	_____	$_____	_____
_____	$_____	_____	$_____	_____
_____	$_____	_____	$_____	_____
_____	$_____	_____	$_____	_____
Necessities (estimated)	$_____	_____	$_____	_____
Beauty or barbershop (estimated)	$_____	_____	$_____	_____
Entertainment (estimated)	$_____	_____	$_____	_____
Items from Pocket Size Tablet	$_____	_____	$_____	_____

TOTAL ABOVE: $_____   TOTAL BILLS PAID: $_____   CARRYOVER: $_____

64

PRACTICE WORKSHEET

DATE:_____

INCOME (_____) $_____

INCOME (_____) $_____

INCOME (_____) $_____

(Subtotal) $_____

(Subtract Tithes-10%) $_____

(Subtotal) $_____

(Add last month's Carryover) $_____

(TOTAL) $_____

	Amount Due	*Date Due*	*Amount Paid*	*Date Paid*
_____	$_____	_____	$_____	_____
_____	$_____	_____	$_____	_____
_____	$_____	_____	$_____	_____
_____	$_____	_____	$_____	_____
_____	$_____	_____	$_____	_____
_____	$_____	_____	$_____	_____
_____	$_____	_____	$_____	_____
_____	$_____	_____	$_____	_____
_____	$_____	_____	$_____	_____
Necessities (estimated)	$_____	_____	$_____	_____
Beauty or barbershop (estimated)	$_____	_____	$_____	_____
Entertainment (estimated)	$_____	_____	$_____	_____
Items from Pocket Size Tablet	$_____	_____	$_____	_____

TOTAL ABOVE: $_____   TOTAL BILLS PAID: $_____   CARRYOVER: $_____

PRACTICE WORKSHEET

DATE:_____

INCOME (_____) $_____

INCOME (_____) $_____

INCOME (_____) $_____

(Subtotal) $_____

(Subtract Tithes-10%) $_____

(Subtotal) $_____

(Add last month's Carryover) $_____

(TOTAL) $_____

	Amount Due	*Date Due*	*Amount Paid*	*Date Paid*
_____	$_____	_____	$_____	_____
_____	$_____	_____	$_____	_____
_____	$_____	_____	$_____	_____
_____	$_____	_____	$_____	_____
_____	$_____	_____	$_____	_____
_____	$_____	_____	$_____	_____
_____	$_____	_____	$_____	_____
_____	$_____	_____	$_____	_____
_____	$_____	_____	$_____	_____
Necessities (estimated)	$_____	_____	$_____	_____
Beauty or barbershop (estimated)	$_____	_____	$_____	_____
Entertainment (estimated)	$_____	_____	$_____	_____
Items from Pocket Size Tablet	$_____	_____	$_____	_____

TOTAL ABOVE: $_____   TOTAL BILLS PAID: $_____   CARRYOVER: $_____

66

PRACTICE WORKSHEET

DATE:_____

INCOME (_____) $_____

INCOME (_____) $_____

INCOME (_____) $_____

(Subtotal) $_____

(Subtract Tithes-10%) $_____

(Subtotal) $_____

(Add last month's Carryover) $_____

(TOTAL) $_____

	Amount Due	_Date Due_	_Amount Paid_	_Date Paid_
_____	$_____	_____	$_____	_____
_____	$_____	_____	$_____	_____
_____	$_____	_____	$_____	_____
_____	$_____	_____	$_____	_____
_____	$_____	_____	$_____	_____
_____	$_____	_____	$_____	_____
_____	$_____	_____	$_____	_____
_____	$_____	_____	$_____	_____
_____	$_____	_____	$_____	_____
Necessities (estimated)	$_____	_____	$_____	_____
Beauty or barbershop (estimated)	$_____	_____	$_____	_____
Entertainment (estimated)	$_____	_____	$_____	_____
Items from Pocket Size Tablet	$_____	_____	$_____	_____

TOTAL ABOVE: $_____   TOTAL BILLS PAID: $_____   CARRYOVER: $_____

67

PRACTICE WORKSHEET

DATE:_____

INCOME (_____) $_____

INCOME (_____) $_____

INCOME (_____) $_____

(Subtotal) $_____

(Subtract Tithes-10%) $_____

(Subtotal) $_____

(Add last month's Carryover) $_____

(TOTAL) $_____

	Amount Due	_Date Due_	_Amount Paid_	_Date Paid_
_____	$_____	_____	$_____	_____
_____	$_____	_____	$_____	_____
_____	$_____	_____	$_____	_____
_____	$_____	_____	$_____	_____
_____	$_____	_____	$_____	_____
_____	$_____	_____	$_____	_____
_____	$_____	_____	$_____	_____
_____	$_____	_____	$_____	_____
_____	$_____	_____	$_____	_____
Necessities (estimated)	$_____	_____	$_____	_____
Beauty or barbershop (estimated)	$_____	_____	$_____	_____
Entertainment (estimated)	$_____	_____	$_____	_____
Items from Pocket Size Tablet	$_____	_____	$_____	_____

TOTAL ABOVE: $_____   TOTAL BILLS PAID: $_____   CARRYOVER: $_____

68

PRACTICE WORKSHEET

DATE:_____

INCOME (_____) $_____

INCOME (_____) $_____

INCOME (_____) $_____

(Subtotal) $_____

(Subtract Tithes-10%) $_____

(Subtotal) $_____

(Add last month's Carryover) $_____

(TOTAL) $_____

	Amount Due	*Date Due*	*Amount Paid*	*Date Paid*
_____	$_____	_____	$_____	_____
_____	$_____	_____	$_____	_____
_____	$_____	_____	$_____	_____
_____	$_____	_____	$_____	_____
_____	$_____	_____	$_____	_____
_____	$_____	_____	$_____	_____
_____	$_____	_____	$_____	_____
_____	$_____	_____	$_____	_____
_____	$_____	_____	$_____	_____
_____	$_____	_____	$_____	_____
_____	$_____	_____	$_____	_____
_____	$_____	_____	$_____	_____
Items from Pocket Size Tablet	$_____	_____	$_____	_____

TOTAL ABOVE: $_____   TOTAL BILLS PAID: $_____   CARRYOVER: $_____

PRACTICE WORKSHEET

DATE:_____

INCOME (_____) $_____

INCOME (_____) $_____

INCOME (_____) $_____

(Subtotal) $_____

(Subtract Tithes-10%) $_____

(Subtotal) $_____

(Add last month's Carryover) $_____

(TOTAL) $_____

	Amount Due	_Date Due_	_Amount Paid_	_Date Paid_
_____	$_____	_____	$_____	_____
_____	$_____	_____	$_____	_____
_____	$_____	_____	$_____	_____
_____	$_____	_____	$_____	_____
_____	$_____	_____	$_____	_____
_____	$_____	_____	$_____	_____
_____	$_____	_____	$_____	_____
_____	$_____	_____	$_____	_____
_____	$_____	_____	$_____	_____
_____	$_____	_____	$_____	_____
_____	$_____	_____	$_____	_____
_____	$_____	_____	$_____	_____
Items from Pocket Size Tablet	$_____	_____	$_____	_____

TOTAL ABOVE: $_____   TOTAL BILLS PAID: $_____   CARRYOVER: $_____

PRACTICE WORKSHEET

DATE:_____

INCOME (_____) $_____

INCOME (_____) $_____

INCOME (_____) $_____

(Subtotal) $_____

(Subtract Tithes-10%) $_____

(Subtotal) $_____

(Add last month's Carryover) $_____

(TOTAL) $_____

	Amount Due	Date Due	Amount Paid	Date Paid
_____	$_____	_____	$_____	_____
_____	$_____	_____	$_____	_____
_____	$_____	_____	$_____	_____
_____	$_____	_____	$_____	_____
_____	$_____	_____	$_____	_____
_____	$_____	_____	$_____	_____
_____	$_____	_____	$_____	_____
_____	$_____	_____	$_____	_____
_____	$_____	_____	$_____	_____
_____	$_____	_____	$_____	_____
_____	$_____	_____	$_____	_____
_____	$_____	_____	$_____	_____
Items from Pocket Size Tablet	$_____	_____	$_____	_____

TOTAL ABOVE: $_____   TOTAL BILLS PAID: $_____   CARRYOVER: $_____

71

PRACTICE WORKSHEET

DATE:_____

INCOME (_____) $_____

INCOME (_____) $_____

INCOME (_____) $_____

(Subtotal) $_____

(Subtract Tithes-10%) $_____

(Subtotal) $_____

(Add last month's Carryover) $_____

(TOTAL) $_____

	Amount Due	_Date Due_	_Amount Paid_	_Date Paid_
_____	$_____	_____	$_____	_____
_____	$_____	_____	$_____	_____
_____	$_____	_____	$_____	_____
_____	$_____	_____	$_____	_____
_____	$_____	_____	$_____	_____
_____	$_____	_____	$_____	_____
_____	$_____	_____	$_____	_____
_____	$_____	_____	$_____	_____
_____	$_____	_____	$_____	_____
_____	$_____	_____	$_____	_____
_____	$_____	_____	$_____	_____
_____	$_____	_____	$_____	_____
Items from Pocket Size Tablet	$_____	_____	$_____	_____

TOTAL ABOVE: $_____   TOTAL BILLS PAID: $_____   CARRYOVER: $_____

PRACTICE WORKSHEET

DATE:_____

INCOME (_____) $_____

INCOME (_____) $_____

INCOME (_____) $_____

(Subtotal) $_____

(Subtract Tithes-10%) $_____

(Subtotal) $_____

(Add last month's Carryover) $_____

(TOTAL) $_____

	Amount Due	_Date Due_	_Amount Paid_	_Date Paid_
_____	$_____	_____	$_____	_____
_____	$_____	_____	$_____	_____
_____	$_____	_____	$_____	_____
_____	$_____	_____	$_____	_____
_____	$_____	_____	$_____	_____
_____	$_____	_____	$_____	_____
_____	$_____	_____	$_____	_____
_____	$_____	_____	$_____	_____
_____	$_____	_____	$_____	_____
_____	$_____	_____	$_____	_____
_____	$_____	_____	$_____	_____
_____	$_____	_____	$_____	_____
Items from Pocket Size Tablet	$_____	_____	$_____	_____

TOTAL ABOVE: $_____   TOTAL BILLS PAID: $_____   CARRYOVER: $_____

<u>EXAMPLES</u>

ADDITIONAL NOTES ON CARRYOVER

The "CARRYOVER" entry is the last entry on your worksheet and will be carried over to the next worksheet, even if it is in the negative. Again, if your carryover happens to be in the negative, do not be discouraged, eventually this will change. After you have many carryovers, and finally a large amount of money to be carried over, what's next? This is the place we desire to reach, this is our goal: having a large amount of money and having to determine how it will be managed. Do you have a year's worth of rent/mortgage, car payments, utilities, transportation, food and other necessities in savings? Do you remember what happened when the government shutdown and companies failed? People lost their jobs, homes, cars and other valuables because they were not prepared to take care of themselves. You can prepare yourself to avoid the devastation that was experienced by those who were not prepared for the shutdown; now is the time to prepare. Use your carryover wisely so that you can be prepared to take care of yourself for months and years to come. You do not have to fail, and you do not have to shut down.

74

The following are examples (estimated) for you to consider; however, you have the final say over your finances.

You work 40 miles away from home and spend $380.00 per month for gas. You changed jobs and now work 10 miles away from home and spend $120.00 per month for gas. You now have $260.00 to add to your carryover. This can be considered a raise; look on the bright side.

What are you going to do with the raise of $260.00 per month? You can keep it in the carryover for as long as you like. Next month you will have this $260.00 plus another $260.00 for that month and so on. Can you imagine having to add to your carryover $260.00 twelve times? When you leave the raise in the carryover of $260.00 per month for 12 months, by the end of 12 months, you will have $3,120.00 in your carryover. If you decide to take the raise away from the carryover, how often will you take it away and how will you use it? Would you use the $260.00 monthly raise to pay off other bills, to purchase necessary insurances, to take vacations, to open an emergency fund or a savings account?

How would you use your raise of $260.00 per month, the money you saved on gas? List ways you might use your raise:

1.

2.

3.

4.

5.

You are not required to spend money just because you have it. You can keep adding money to the money you have and be prepared for the next shutdown of any agency or place of employment. Remember, you do not have to participate in loss or be negatively affected by any shutdown.

Here is another example: If you had a car payment of $500.00 per month and now it is paid in full. Will you keep the monthly payment in your carryover? Will you save it for a down payment on your next vehicle? Will you put it in an emergency fund? Will you pay off other bills?

What will you do with the raise of $500.00 per month, since you no longer have a car payment?

1.

2.

3.

4.

5.

Learn to discipline yourself by not spending just because you have money or just because you cannot seem to resist buying certain items. You should be able to live at least one year and pay all bills without receiving a paycheck. Once you are able to save for one year of provisions, move on to saving for two years, three years and keep adding the years. If you apply yourself, you can do it. It has been done and it works. Will you accept the challenge to apply the principles that I have shared and to start using the pocket size tablet and worksheets in this workbook?

77

CONCLUSION

My ability to be organized, along with a commitment to follow the principles I have shared with you in this workbook, has tremendously enriched my life in many ways. I pray your experience will be as enriched, fulfilled and as successful as mine. I am concluding with a prayer for those who believe in and desire prayer.

"My heavenly Father, I bless your most holy and awesome name. I worship you and honor your presence. You mean more than life to me. I thank you for loving me, protecting me, and for holding me dear to your heart. The Bible tells me that your plan for me is a good plan, and that your plan is for my good, to do me good all the days of my life and not evil. Your plan is for me to receive the promise of a good future and a good end. Your plan is for the earth to be inhabited with mankind; those who will fulfill your plan. I open my heart to you and ask that you impart unto me godly wisdom, knowledge, understanding, skills and abilities that will enable me to carry out your plan for my life.

I give myself to you and depend on the leading, teaching and comfort of the Holy Spirit. Thank you for being such a merciful, patient and loving Father. I thank you in advance for giving me grace to be merciful, patient and loving to those who show me love and mercy and to those who do not. Thank you for providing everything I need, and more than I need. The Bible tells me that it is your pleasure to give me the kingdom. You have always been my help, strength and protector. You have done more for me than I could ever say. What can I render to you for all you have done for me? I give you myself, my life and all that I have. Use me, Lord, to fulfill your plan and purpose for my life. I surrender all, as I wait to hear from you, in Jesus' name. Amen!"

ABOUT THE AUTHOR

Dr. Sharon Lee Graham

Dr. Sharon Lee Graham is an author, business woman, and pastor. She strives to do business and ministry in the spirit of excellence and believes in keeping her word, even if it hurts or causes her to put forth an extra effort. She emphasizes that operating in the spirit of excellence and keeping your word are two of the most important things you can do if you expect to gain respect and trust in ministry or business.

Dr. Graham is a native of Chicago, Illinois, and has lived in the state of Illinois most of her life. She attended schools in the Chicago area and majored in the field of business. Dr. Graham has worked for numerous companies throughout the years, including the Federal Aviation Administration (FAA). She retired from the FAA with more than 37 years of public service. Due to the training received, she has held various positions and is well-rounded in many areas of aviation and business. She is fully aware of how the training and experiences in life have prepared her for the future; they are the stepping stones that continue leading her to higher heights in her business and ministry.

In 2000, while working full-time and overseeing two non-profit ministries, Dr. Graham attended the Christian Satellite Bible University, Chicago, Illinois, where she majored in Christian Counseling. In 2001 she received her degree of Bachelor of Christian Education in Christian Counseling graduating class valedictorian, Summa Cum Laude; in 2002 she received her Master Degree graduating Summa Cum Laude, and in 2004 she received her Doctoral Degree graduating Summa Cum Laude. She continued her education and earned her Doctoral Degree in Theology in 2006, graduating Summa Cum Laude. These degrees were earned through the International Apostolic University of Grace and Truth, Indianapolis, Indiana (IAUGT).

Dr. Graham has held the position of assistant pastor and has sat under the teachings of profound Bible scholars. Receiving her first license for ministry in 1966, she was publicly ordained in 1995. She is the Pastor of Life In Christ~Christ In Me Ministries, Inc., (April 1997), and president of Sharon Graham Ministries, Inc., (April 2003), located in a western suburb of Chicago.

Dr. Graham is the sole proprietor of Dr. Sharon Lee Graham Productions, a company that produces written materials, and has expectations of expanding the company by producing visual and audio materials as well. She loves to study and teach what she has learned. Dr. Graham seeks to motivate others by giving them a boost of encouragement and by pushing them forward and causing them to press ahead in the Spirit to the next level of where they are supposed to be.

She has written two other books that have been published, "How to Survive a Marriage with a Non-Christian Spouse," and a workbook "Your Personal Challenge". Dr. Graham believes you must use what you have or you lose it. She said, "I am going to redeem the time and recover all. I do not have time to waste anything."

CONTACT INFORMATION:

Website - www.sharonleegraham.com

Email - drslgproductions@sbcglobal.net

www.ingramcontent.com/pod-product-compliance
Lightning Source LLC
Chambersburg PA
CBHW050240220326
41598CB00047B/7467